Watch Us Pass

Robert Canzoneri

Watch Us Pass

Ohio State University Press

For Antonina

What soul can sit untainted
In so strong a world?

Acknowledgments

Acknowledgment is gratefully made of the permission granted to include the following previously published poems in the present collection: "Spring Comes from Under," *The Lyric*, Spring, 1959; "The Day the Cold Came," *Red Clay Reader III*, 1966; "On Driving North in May," *Sewanee Review*, Vol. LXXI, No. 2 (April-June, 1963); "The Lines Are Drawn," *Per/Se*, Winter, 1967/68; "When Warmth Withdraws," *Poetry Southeast, 1950–70*; "One Lion, Once," *Saturday Review*, September 17, 1963; "A Puppy Tongue" and "Obit," *The Miscellany*, December, 1965; "The Unloved" and "The Web and the Wing," *New Campus Writing IV*, 1962; "Mississippi: That Grand Old State of Mind," *Mississippi Poetry Journal*, Spring, 1958; "Discovery of America," *Colorado Quarterly*, Autumn, 1964; "Sandstorm," *Saturday Review*, January 1, 1963; "Her Mind Was a Blade" and "The Path Impounded," *Northeast 1966*; "Passioni," *Epos*, Winter, 1964/65; "As Artist," *Four Quarters*, Vol. XV, No. 4 (May, 1966); "To William Faulkner," *Poetry Southeast, 1950–70*; "On Realizing a Generation," *Discourse*, Summer, 1964; "To My Father, As We Grow Old," *Poetry Southeast, 1950–70*; and "To a Celebrated Beauty Dying Young" and "Where One Went Down," *Red Clay Reader III*, 1966.

R. C.

Contents

Part I

Cryptic the Device

Spring Comes From Under

Spring comes from under, swells
in the seed, not cloud; shares dirt smells.

Ground just unfrozen will upfling
blue daisies so small that anything
as loud as dead grass stalks
catches more attention, balks
the spring-seeking eye. They wait
one who must stoop to dig for bait
or garden plot, but they are there
to see, four-petaled, bare,
cut from one piece; their blue and birth
less of sky and air than of earth.

Spring comes from under, swells
in the seed, not cloud; shares earth smells.

Pine Pollen

(Louisiana, 1963)

Spurred stars
Of sprung stamen
Spatter the aging night of pine,
Spelling spring,
Spilling spring
In drifts
And puffs
Of yellow.

      Sun
Rays run
In shifts through needles
Spotting sperm.

Spraying sperm,
Wind-fluid soughs
Off clouds
Of stuff so fine
The air is pale
And visible.

Prodigal pines
Dust our shoes,
Scar our path.

Scud

Of yellow dud
Seeks sidewalk cracks
And crevices;
Dying, it sifts
Beneath our feet.
We stop, we breathe,
While air has life,
Excess.

Our red car dulls with life,
And prints of hands on red
Unfurled
Gather and spread
A scar,
A star,
Each point a spine,
Each joint
A bright whorled
Yellow
Sign.

To a Campus Tree in Spring,
Seen Out a Second Story Window

Only your middle shows from here, green starred
Big branches, solid trunk. I climbed you raw,
As a savage boy, hugged your rough bark.
But, older now, I'll climb you felled and sawed,
Walk up stairways under a shingled roof
More solid than your sky of summer leaves,
Four floors above root ground to our highest room.
And if your twig-top green still higher lives
Than I, I'll tell you of less academic
Buildings built of sand-lime fusions, steel,
Your wood, and the clay you cling to baked to brick:
Structures that stand more than ten times as tall.
They know of soil: to sweep; of rain: to shed.
We let you stain our rooftop with your shade.

The Day the Cold Came

Football lights drew bugs of summer;
where were the southward geese?
Apple sprung to bloom again, and gum trees
leaved, the damned instinctive fools.
Gardeners cursed the burlap
weekly rotting by azaleas
under no frigid siege.

Our craving had the edge
of fresh tub ice.
The midnight bark of shivering dogs
struck us as nice.
Winter's dark discomfort
of bulky clothes
we lusted, and approaching numbness
from our toes.

The day it came we dared it. After work
we walked the early dark on sidewalks, jerked
off our gloves and barked our knuckles hard
against the tight tree bark—and then forgot
that kind of foolishness.

                    Under the graphic
mercury vapor lamps we saw a man
of pumps working an anti-freeze device

long-hosed at a lock-jawed car.

Name

the perversity by which the moon incensed
us, rising tropic yellow like a lion.
We stopped and stared it up in cold denial,
watched it pale to silver, chilled, convinced.
We flipped it like a dollar over our shoulder.
Nobody, we could swear, was ever colder.

Cold Spell

Blood rose soon in the redbud—quite
Artless to yield to such careless art,
Now to bleed unabashed in the open sight
Of a sun withdrawn except for light.

But the dogwood drew its blossoms tight.
Now only the bold, intrigued by sleight,
Hold cupped and crossed, stunned, half-apart,
Frigid, lip-bruised, stiff and white.

On Driving North in May

We drive backward into spring
(Spring is the backward thing),

Drive north from where green leaves are grown
To where leaf green has lightly shown

In leaf buds clenched with fright and chill
Knowing a night of frost can kill.

Though we could miss the mid-year heat
By driving on in cold deceit,

We will return for summer's prime,
Abide diminished autumntime:

Since it will come, there's little reason
To drive into the final season.

Low Ground

Those three dark days buried by storm
While low black clouds were clogging our eyes,
Nothing about us was dry or warm
Or presaged light from open skies.
What had begun nothing could raise
For three dark days.

                    But now it is done.
The mountain most often hidden in haze
(What to us were rains to it were snows)
Stands white and high, sharp to our sight
Where four in a light plane crashed and froze.

The Lines Are Drawn

The lines are drawn,
However much they shift,
Between the wet and dry,
The rock and what's adrift.

Shells seem discrete,
However glazed with doubt
That what we see within
Is stuff that's not without.

Boards show that trees
May stand after they fall,
But windows frame the fact
Of nothing in a wall,

No fence ungapped,
No line drawn not to shift
Between dead and alive,
The rock and what's adrift.

When Warmth Withdraws

When warmth withdraws
And rain reverts to sleet,
Treacherous the laws
That rule our feet.

When heat dims out
And air is flocked with snow,
Cold and sure our doubt
Which way to go.

When warmth denies
And dew distorts to frost,
Cryptic the device
That writes us lost.

Part II

Both Head and Tail

One Lion, Once

Ho, Androcles!
What do you say went on
From when the lion scratched off in the dust
Toward you as meat and bone
And, roaring to his lean and hungry guts
The end of grumbling wait,
Bore down? What shifted in those preying eyes
As, closing, you grew featured
And the features made a face? What lies
Would not reach truth too late
But failed the heated lion's sight, as face
Became not one man's meat,
But Androcles?
We could ask Plato, looking back, to place
The abstract qualities
Of this into a scheme: how many rungs
Of love a beast can seize
In one great charge, to land (with rasping lungs
And flesh starved to his bones)
Muzzling like a milk-fed cat at ease
Against you on your knees.

A Puppy Tongue

A puppy tongue that licks and puppy eyes
speak with a clarity that words and sighs
aspire to; impulsive tongue, teeth that gnaw
on knuckles with such careful gauge that draw-
ing blood's unthought of draw instead strong hands
down silky puppy sides, impulsive and
uncrushing careful as the dog. What song
can sing love into being better? Strong
language this, and gross a puppy's size
for those impelled to love, loath to grow wise.

Obit

He went in for sports
chasing imports on our street,
the green Volkswagen and orange Dauphine.
Fords were not debarked
but a road-bound yacht he'd mark without assail,
take in his stride
as though their fantails flew identical flags.

The visiting MG ripped low and white
Bronx cheering into sight; better than sport,
a mobile bone ripe for burial if caught.
But against its bite his bark was much too frail.
The rites were on the road;
a Packard classic
(his carcass was flattered)
officiated.

The Unloved

When I would squat by holes and piles of dirt
crumbling clods, ready to insert
bare roots of shrubs, she'd soil my vegetable dreams:
this adolescent dog approaching albino
would worm under my arm with motive I know
too but bury in pride, curl both head
and tail toward me begging to be fed
love at both extremes.

Neither was an end unto itself, or
small dogs one might do as well for;
a car front struck her fore part like a match
that spurts red fire and dies, curdled a batch
of blood out from one end and knocked
oval feces out the other. Shocked,
arrested at the waste, I swore a herbist
vow; but now I felt the still unserviced
bitch for lack of pulse and breath. I coiled
her limp into a hamper, saw it soiled
with drying blood. She stiffened in a curl,
never having learned a nicer girl
could hope to stay unspaded, yet behave.
With too much heat I dug a rounded grave.

Gulls on Plowed Ground

Mushrooms once grew here on open fields
Wild, but new-plowed the old acreage yields
Gulls in a cluster, a patch on the brown:
Seagulls grubbing where nothing can drown,
Placid and gray as oysters in silt.

Hung high between ocean and bay, they tilt
Down to these clods; and now gulls have found
Breakers are colder than broken ground.

Landsmen nearby should have nothing to say—
Bound in peninsula ways by the bay,
Plodding and dry, taking shelter from rain—
But they harbor a cry, and the cry harbors pain:
Open your white-under breast-curved wings
Wide to the skies! Crowd the ocean with wings!

The Web and the Wing

Rapt,
blundering on, a flung
bluebottle fly, I sing
between lax webs crosshung,
onward. I am the wing,
touched but unstung: dared,
I swing and stumble hard,
flop in and through the flared
elastic net. Unscarred
but scared, unstrung, I drop
bravado, turn and rip
wide of the web: trip
an unseen trap, and stop.
Wrapped.

Part III

More Than Our Bodies

To a College Girl

Nearsighted girl with tiny teeth,
I fear that glasses, awkward, cold,
Block many a deal for aging full
Fresh skins like yours, unpassioned breaths,
Not yet formed faces.

Yet how a turning of your head
Turns distant pity into dread
Of ancient graces!

In profile, shielded baffled eyes
Seem shrinking from some half-seen buyer;
Full face they draw his doubtful blur
To love's complete myopia
Through deep showcases.

Two

Both were so shy
Their only tie
Was bedded, hooded dark delight.

Pity their plight
And curse the night
She wept and could not tell him why.

To a Disillusioned Young Husband

The touch of any such must be clung to:
the stiff rim of off rhyme may ring
melody clear to senses ears are hung to:

true rhyme unminded is a doubtful thing
snared only in a drum; sweet's tainted still
though beat from stalks, trapped and kettled; wing-

flight's not wingless, fights its lifting foil
through drag of air; unhampered speed must crest
as light, and light's engrossed to heat if held

as wives must be. If life is to exist,
hold love though fleshed; loved flesh, though clumsy, trust.

To My Wife, An Invitation

Let us toss love and us into the tub,
use lye and truth to bleach the deepest dye
(dyeing is cheap: eschew it). You may scrub
accumulated dirt while ruthless I
scrape off all false designs and fancies, rub
out the print of adolescent dream-and-sigh,
the stain of song, the movie gloss and pub-
lic gilt. Spread it and us in sun to dry.

Don't falter, fearing love will go with lint:
count threads, feel textures with strong fingers, taste,
inhale essential odors, turn the glint
of naked eyes on seams. Indulge no haste,
but test it hem and nap. Still when we're wrapped
we'll find more than our bodies overlapped.

Too Tired for Love We Lie

Too tired, too tired for love we lie unbent
In gravely parallel pressed-coil depressions.
Quiescent all our ergs and urges, spent;
But, stirred, arouse enough to raise a question:
Must love be active now or not at all?
Postpone and perish would be too ironic;
Our carnal fear spurs us toward carnival
(Passion's acute, but fear of death is chronic)
And muscles move themselves. In spite of all
Lax fingers faintly touch: love lies platonic.

Temblor

The night the bed shook us
Inertia held us high
and bottomless.
Held breath lets out no cry,

Yet flaws were in the crust
Of earth, and, eyes like owls',
We grew there to distrust
Deeply its bowels.

Dust settled to the doubt,
On grounds of love,
Beneath might prove such fault
As we were not above.

But quick before a look
Could show us tame,
We made a fist and shook
The bed and all its frame.

Part IV

At Their Age

Tony and Nina

Christmas, 1958

Strung silver bells cling down your spine
And ring till tips of fingers shine
Tinsel ice afire with light:
Santa reds firecracker bright,
Dark cedar greens, blue ten-belows,
And whites whiter than whitest snows.

Cheeks chimneybrick red, holly hair,
You're needle-skinned, frost-stung, aware:
Cold caroled ears, star-pointed eyes,
Windows wide upon night skies,
As Christmas sifts as soft as snows
From tip down to your mistletoes.

Cleaning Up

(Nina)

At her age, she doesn't dip
Her hands into the sink,
But stands at arm-stretch
Dripping suds, and talks:
"My teacher's the nicest thing!
I mean, she has to get mad,
But she always says she's sorry
Afterwards."
Shouldering hair from her eyes,
She squints at a foaming dish
And then straight-arms it clean.
"Some teachers
Just leave their yells in the children."

Part V

To Get to the Other Side

Mississippi

That Grand Old State of Mind

(Citizen, tell me,
What is your favorite tree?
"Magnolia is the bes',
Ah guess.")
Unlike oaks
Magnolias are a hoax
Of expense
That doesn't quite convince;
Not so coarse
As pines and sycamores,
Nor so trim
As poplar girls who swim
To stay slim,
Magnolia matrons corset
Up like hoarse
Harridans whose sole defense
Is pretense,
Whose gaudy brooch provokes
Canvas jokes.
(Now that you've heard from me,
What is your favorite tree?
"Ah tol' yuh.
Magnolia.")

49

On Crossing the Kentucky River Bridge
Near Lawrenceburg

You boastful backwoods dullard, Dan'l Boone,
busting your buckskin with muscle bulge,
don't squeeze our slender biceps down the bone
within your frontier fist, and shrug.

Our skulls have sapped our bodies. Strength is latent
in intellect, in reining pulse
and senses sturdily. Equilibrating
ears are ours, and heady poise.

Sure, in silent shoes you stalked the b'ar
and rifled arrowed redskin toughs;
you rafted rivers on a log, rode bark
bareback through ragged troughs.

But now might you not fear to ford the stream,
dizzied by depths beneath a concrete track
wrought high between your ridges, cowed by strum
of tires, panicked by trucks?

Pit brawn against bridge, set stealth against steep,
battle our bears of metal—
you lose. Our hardihood is to be weak
but not unsettled.

Discovery of America

Those who cross to get to the other side
Sandwich it between meals. As they ride
Out of sight high overhead and gone,
We pioneers in covered station wagons
Crawl the surface mounting always west
Through plains with roadside doe and fawn,
Up pine-black hills whose valleys sag
With coddled buffalo. The crest
And dip of moonlit waste provide
The swift soft thud of rabbits suicidal,
A slaughterous tradition kept by chance.
We taste the ice of glacial air and dance
Fantastic doodles down a canyon wall.
We are the rubber-rolling train, the tidal
Lag—wry anti-tourist sycophants
Driven to new childhood by expanse,
To candid trust that snapshots will enthrall
Our one vast land, discovered small by small.

The California Gardener Speaks

All morning long a rainbow bent its arc
Against chaos and cloud on Menlo Park
As though God's middle garden man had spread
Hibiscus, marigolds, a bluebell bed
Against gray western dirt. (We like our land
Worked bare where plants drawn up from loam expand
To earthly flowers.) The sun rose toward past noon
Through high white clouds and sky, until too soon
Color was sapped, at least from landward sight.
Touching all day this avid soil it might
Have taken root, we say and half believe.
The mistiest illusions may deceive
Fools into idleness; but, heaven knows,
We have to grub from ground what color grows.

Sandstorm

They laid the concrete, but they left the sand.
And what can one expect of desert roads,
Even labeled U.S. on a shield
Too small to hide behind? Our view of land
As placid waste was qualified by loads
Blown up as cloud, as blinding scatter-shot.
We bluffed against it, planning how to wield
Our little water, should the sand reduce
Us to survival tactics on the spot.
Our windshield flecked and pocked. The least misuse
Of wind is hell where everything is loose.

Crossing the Lower Bay

The bay itself had been blue;
Kept pools lay flat in rigid dikes
Where the bridge lapsed
And a raised black road laid an obtuse angle through.
Ahead the factory exhausted
Distant white smoke from dead salt white,
Its framed reflection opaque green as oil.
A plot of sluggish red had lost
All but the penciled outline of a hill.
In the wires overhead, a gull—
The feathers and salt-cured hide, the hull
Of a gull caught like a weathered kite.

Bahama Reef

Blue, blue-green to coral
reef-depth rife of color
slow rolls below, a fanlike
unfolding light-flaw in the flat Atlantic,
a translucent stain, a pastel glass
inset whose edges water galls.

Say engines fail; shall we feather our craft
into clarity, glide a down loop
to shock tiled water, lie black fractured?
Pray God we spare that pool.

The Substance of Things Unseen

He sees it, odd moments, over Africa,
A splendid skinless balloonful
Of hope expanded and faith
An exhalation over
Africa, magnet of missionaries
And home of Hemingway's
Green hills, his snowpeak
And spot of frozen leopard,
Hung over high with unbodied guts
And sightless souls—
Elan of well-gunned wildebeest,
Converts, converters,
And dying hunters.
He sees it, odd moments, and hears at home
The spent breath of believers
Form on lips confined as bone
Dry bubbles of belief.
What sustains it, what it sustains,
He cannot say, nor how one can define
So surfaceless a wind
Which neither blown nor blowing moves
Some men.

Full House

The Family Gathered for the News

Edited: We're swept past open
Stalls of stolen goods, the hope
Of slender bright hot Vietnamese.
Bills fan as though to make a breeze;
We're slowed to watch swift fingers riffle these.

A crowded courtroom scene is graced
By the Premier, ascetic-faced
And aptly thin about the waist,
A sign to other men whose lust
Is profit-based his army threatens justice.

Two bow, but one is singled out:
Round cheeks; there is no room for doubt.
Chinese. War profiteer. A man
Of his own time, whose image can
Be seen in Maine on sets made in Japan.

There stands his wife. The sentence said,
He lifts his child high as his head.
Next episode will show him dead.
By rule we're bound to let it pass,
Though arms can break through any pane of glass.

57

Part VI

Show Me Some End

My Last Day Off

No more give rope enough to me.
To hang about at loose ends ties
Days into knots; the rest is lies.
Time is most taut when feet are free.

Freeway

A bird-cloud flung against a gust,
splayed its density and receded;
weightier, wadded itself downwind,
black, wing-wrought, and unimpeded.

A man aligned in an outside lane
glimpsed the birds and, swerving, burst
across the curb, through ditch and fence
square into bird-field mud. He cursed

(spinning his wheels for all to see
who dared) simultaneity.

Young Faculty

Having goosed its gods in a cubbyhole
and giggled our faces sore,
we emerge to a campus new with elm leaves.

Ghost grins disgrace the study
as gone as last night's drunk,
and three girls, sleeveless, walk the grass abreast.

Office pokers at idols,
we gauge the aftergall
where new green grows and girls go lightly dressed.

Carolyn Robed

Though she assumes a one-day black cocoon,
Graduation is not to butterfly
(However much her words outdance, defy
The pen, her voice transforms, outsings the tune).

Nor is the robe a shroud in which to die
And resurrect, though others gladly drown,
Assured new life whose names are written down
On sheepskin rolls above. She will not lie

Inert or in hope. She knows robes may try
To bury her or lull her to some sigh
For miracle, but knows that like the sky,
The shade of trees, a house, a skull, an eye,

They serve to be looked out from and to win
Beyond, grown by one day more Carolyn.

To One Appalled at the P-H-D

No nouveau niche,
This function which
Is now degreed;
Though poorly fee'd,
Hoary its age.
The scholar, sage
And thorough, must
The reaping gust
Of genius trail,
Must glean what gale
Blew over, list
What thresher missed.
So, was it not,
In Camelot?
When Lancelot
And steed had struck
With lance and luck
Like living thunder,
Who thought to wonder
At knaves who came,
Measured his aim,
Sighted his course,
And records kept
Of all they swept
After his horse?

Her Mind Was a Blade

Her mind was a blade of steel
    without a handle.
It glittered as it played
    at deadly random.

It spun and shot through air
    with cold precision,
But where it flicked would not
    be her decision.

She watched it jab and probe,
    never at rest.
She stood and let it lob
    off both her breasts.

Man with an Axiom to Grind

He took a bath twice a day
And washed his body oils away,
Which bared him to the fact that, oddly,
Though cleanly, true, was next to godly,
Yet cleanly was as cleanly did.
And what he knew he cleanly hid.

A stitch in time caused his surmise
The cream it was that didn't rise.
Horse sense, he swears, spurred him to think,
Led him from water and made him drink.
Now he believes with both his eyes
Each tub on its own bottom lies.

Every dogmatic has his day,
The saying goes, and who's to say
He won't draw wealth as well as flies
Oily to bed, oily to rise?

Ends and the Means I Sing

To an End-of-the-Roader

Of course
The end
Is bound up in the means,
Which means
There is no end
Other than means have tended
Toward with shaping force.
(Although
Means that are sly,
Laced
With a lie,
Just may obtain
An unbraced
Momentary gain,
Even so,
Bloody the way,
Bloody the final day.)
But hell,
You who intend
Climactic final scenes,
And such foretell,
Show me some end
That isn't a means
As well.

Part VII

Forays

The Path Impounded

Conscientiously you tend the grounds.
After you have walked your weekly rounds
I see the hired men prune appointed shrubs,
Edge ragged ditches, sod a patch. One grubs
About perennials; another plants
Beds of what flowers in season have a chance.
Without you this would be a wilderness.

Yet what can we in conscience not assess?
Superintending is your job, and one
Must ask what you intend to put upon
Us with this pavement now. The path
We wore astray was but an aftermath:
By chart, terrain, and play of mind we move;
We plot in getting there from here to prove
What way, as things are underfoot, our campus
Walks discover most.

                           Why not just stamp
Us fit for axes, as each fall you blaze
Unplanted trees? Or boldly post some phrase
Designed to give us pause? No; levels, lines,
And wooden forms in trenches are the signs
Our latest route's cut off. It seems you care
Somehow about our soles. But when you dare
Sanction us with concrete, watch us pass
Induced by altered grounds to greener grass.

Passioni

$\times$

The mass
removing place from place
(say, feet from face)
is not more solid
nor more crass
than circumstance times space.

$\div$

The line
dividing false from true
(say, me from you)
is not wider
nor more fine
than someone into who.

$+$

The distance
from one thing to another
(say, a brother)
is not greater
(in this instance)
than father summed with mother.

—

The shade
darkening our sight
(say, black from white)
is not deeper,
more inlaid,
than brilliance minus light.

=

The whole
pervading as the sea
(say, empathy)
as synthesized synecdoche
embraces poles—
thus: me in you makes we.

To My Father, Ex-Italian, Ex-Catholic

Father Columbus risked the world-edge fall.
Compatriot, you braved the old world curse
By walking damned into a plain plank church
On papish trapdoors lettered: HELL.

Bored cabin boys cruising at thirty knots
Litter the Atlantic with science-fiction pulp,
Plan how to plumb sky depths by flying up.
I falter at familiar church door mats.

Now, would Columbus hold our sphere's a ball
And damn our newer seekers of new worlds,
Preach earth as all? Will you forbid forays
Who carpeted the ancient site of hell?

Premises and the Man

With prickly skin
And swimming eyes
He carefully abstracted
Essence of sin,
And in what guise
Whatever is is acted:

"Feeling comes first,
Then what is taught,
And afterwards comes thinking:
Man moved by thirst
Searches by thought
For drink sanctioned for drinking.
Sin is reversal, then,
Or some improper linking."

Yet as he felt
Righteous, indeed
Thought righteous too,
And, godly, knelt
To goodly seed
Planted for once so true
In fertile ground
When he was young,

Blithely his tongue
Was tasting weeds
Sown by no one,
Green and bitter as rue.
Part of him grew
Frightened, undone
And strangely fired,
For he was bound
Beyond his skin,
Out of his mind
On untaught sin
No thought designed
Nor conscious cell desired—
As though it were
Pure Sequence that required
Non sequitur.

Dead Reckoning

Somewhere in the Universe

My willful run
being my own,
I steer straight on
admonishing one
who veers and is gone,
lamenting some
aimlessly spun
eccentric circles down
inert as stone;
assured and swift alone
of all, I fly—
and smile to see the sun
scribbling my name
against a shifting sky.

Part VIII

As Artist

Pathétique

(Impressions of a Painting by John C. Craiger)

I

Lily of decease misplaced
In the hand of a live child:
Deceitful lily, white life
Lace, of death the icing.

II

You do not look the same
Through the window of pain
As in surprised eyes
Doubtful in surmise.

III

Between the blight and tout d'abord,
Middle life: the encompassed view
Sieving in pale rich words
The sad essence of *It flew*.

IV

End approaches like an escalator head.
She ceases scrambling downward
And stands still on the treadmill
Silent, deep; unmoving always deathward.

Four Views of a Piano Concert

I

Disconcerted, we forget
the grand piano's reach,
forget what hull affords
heartwood that knuckles shrink from knocking. Watch
it stretch rigid as a frigate
poised on launching boards.

II

The hall has too much space.
Empty seats surround
a shrinking island race
left long ago aground
under a flat white sky.
Applause lost in high
lost air, faded as surf
splash fades at sea, is scattered in a patter per-
fect wash of palm to palm
cliché directed at
the manikin. He swims
erect in view and calm

up to the high strung whale,
whose lower jaw protrudes
white teeth enough to eat
manikin tie and tails.
Silent, manikin broods
as one who waits his whims,
then strikes the whale. What sound!
The plaster sky, the seats
are full, the air's profound,
manikin is man,
the whale is dead, yet lives
aloud through man who gives
the sea plan.

III

Muscled spiders rumble side by side
on fanning legs; intensified
they swell, then leap
sideways a flank
to flank flip-flop
up flat white linking
plats,
white slats,
pick sharp shrill feet
through prickles fit
for beetle heels,
pause enthralled
on shrill
electric bells
spinning web,
spinning,
wobble once

and plunge
prey-pouncing down
stripped steps
to stop,
wait full and sound,
weaving, idling deep,
alert to prance the steeps
above their foot-flanged
muttering, if challenged.

IV

Fingers are perfection: bred of love
in practiced action it is love they breed
beat by beat, note by note and need
by calculated need; bare of glove
and stripped of pose, performing unashamed
as bare-limbed dancers fling bare hands and feet
aflight, rehearsed in freedom, so the fleet
strong fingers rise and leap by love inflamed.

A golden name
hangs on the edge of dusk;
white arms salaam,
whiter the thighs in risk
that genuflect
with deep-skinned counterparts,
that fold unflocked
and fill with wild disports.
Beware the rip,
the tear through dark smooth silk,
beware the creep
through scrim, the shadow sulk,

the leap,
the bundled bulk.

A name in gold
defines the face of night;
white thighs are bold
with dusky thighs in sight.

Bred of love, fingers are perfection;
whitely they dance with ebony reflection.

To a Pseudo-Shelley

The grass seems brightest at the silent hour
Before new day has taken breath, or heat
Distended air, or sun dispelled from flower
The pool of dark about its stamen feet
Deep in the petal cup. It is deceit
To turn the half-light of so fresh a stage
Full on, you cry, in anguish at the beat
Of time's full heart and all that grows with age.

Poet forever young, lie there in dew
And sing as though you knew the earth was made
For sheen and innocence; romantic rue,
Plucked in some noon exposure, savor in shade,
In solitude, in ostentatious sloth.
Then play that you are flame, night is the moth.

The Real

In burgundy velvet coat and glittering pin
He mounted the curving stair
And said (his modulation appropriate, thin),
"Very well, my dear, but spare
Me the sordid details,"

And exited
Down rough lumber steps
Over loose nails;
Flew through the wings;
Flashed splendid
(Glimpsed) past bulb-framed glass;
Came to a void;
And sweating through his makeup
Winced at his hemorrhoids;

    —So flushed with pain that instant
    A vision of the real
    Long-gone tycoon in million-dollar vest
    And genuine glass-cutting diamond pin
    (Perfect, tasteful, hard)
    Walking so,
    Slow, sedate, up handcarved walnut stairs
    And down his velvet-footed halls
    Solid with walnut walls,
    Sweating wet his pure silk underwear—

Wiped clear the ghost
And rushed up to his post behind the set
On cue, however hot,
Slowly to walk down curving stairs
(O chandeliers
Of cheap glass crystal light!)
And moneyed with aplomb fall stiffly right
Before the hackneyed blank:
Most foully shot.
Dying in velvet, putting on heirs, an age
Sank
To bas-relief onstage.

Word Men

For John Ciardi

Facts far too heard
Drop into use
As farce
Or fizz

When undeterred
Word men will goose
The arse
Of Is.

Plot

This minute square of grass singly of green,
glass-flat, clean, uncurved—its hedge,
too, short, trimmed close; blade, stem, and leaf
clipped at the edge of an aboslute:

my flesh feels such care cut near to the nerve,
and sharp is the screech of metal on metal.

As Artist

His eye upon a ruddy tree
Stemmed with berries pale and red
Sees each leaf stiffen into gold,
Sees twigs set high and diamonded
And mounted rubies, rigid, hold
Fixed glints of light immutably.

Why halt this autumn dogwood here
And freeze it living stiff as ice?
How crystallize the passing light?
What is the pupilled artifice
That, graduating, teaches sight
Selection final and severe?

Ciardi

Fog Butcher for the World

On Gibraltar
(God, what rock!)
Trajectory can culminate
In one small pock.
Mark, at closer range
(Shapes
Can change
At any rate)
How the indigenous apes
Can alter
The fundamental whole
By playing ring
Around
Morose
Breastworks and mole:
How sound
And rosy
Is the soul
Prodded prudence
Must extol,
Sing,
Or by some strange
Extrudence

Frigged from cosy
Dead set stone
Bubble
Belch or bellow
As the dawn
Comes up like wonder
Out of childhood
Crossed
And double
Double.

To William Faulkner

Two Weeks After His Death

You stood
(I kept your distance then)
Small and erect, tilting the courthouse square
Into your head,
Pulsing it with your blood.

Even to death
Repulsed,
Today I kept the road despite a grave
Out of the common lot.
No stone yet settled where you lay beneath

Clumps of dry clay,
Shovel carved
Shards of land disturbed; where dust would age
Unmarked,
Your body lay

Biding its decline.
Pulse of your outrage
Blooded my mind.

The Poet Recorded

To Yvor Winters

When you are dead this voice will startle **air**,
Shake off our nightmare of mortality
One moment of insane belief: you there
Palpable, impassive as reality,
As if the flesh were heavy on the bone,
Mind weighty in the skull, and nothing gone.

How now, old mole, canst work i' the earth so fast?
Stir roots and shift our ground, swear out of time
Progeny you never got? Who guessed
Your seed late scattered should inhabit limb
And lung and blood, reconstitute in essence?
Who dreamed of sonship by your word and presence?

Ingenuity, sending this voice
Unbodied in the world, quibbles with death.
Old use and love, choosing beyond all choice,
Dare to translate sound waves into breath.
But by what subtle rite, past all surprise,
Can words transmute to flesh, insight to eyes?

95

Part IX

Our Full Identity

On Realizing a Generation

Up from a page
In which my mind has scanned
An age,
I look—
And find my father's hand
Holding my book.

To My Father, As We Grow Old

Now is your death, to me
Who must die too,
Less to be concealed.
Though death for you
My death will not have healed,
On my bones see
Flesh that already fails,
Follows, and hails
Our full identity.

On Reading of One War, Recalling Another

Catch the shock of boy eyes, wide,
Admitting death whatever war.
Mortal innocents they died,
Leapt to conclude as sons—denied
The hurt their fathers caught, the scar.

To a Celebrated Beauty Dying Young

Woman I never knew,
What was so special in your flesh
Captured with such silken flash
In newsprint pictures—you?

Why does your set file by,
Silent as if sincere,
No matter that you lie
Unshaken and severe?

   Another beauty gone,
   And now I read, again,
   This one was insecure, but real,
   A good and lovely honest witch
   Caught in a phony deal
   And used by every son of a bitch.

What can I add who almost mourn?
Except: If I had known,
You might have had a passing chance
At a more subtle song and dance.

Except (another quick cliché):
Die rather than falsely live—
My rouge for cheeks whose fixed display
Has no alternative.

Where One Went Down

He was brought up blue as veins.
Rains
Cannot obliterate
His fate.
The searchers lugged him clear
Here
Where we are swimming now.
How remarkable that his tongue
Hung
Bloated and dripping wet;
Yet the surface holds us live.
Dare we dive?

For R. M.

We have hovered with uncertain hands
Over your death,
With untouching fingers, tilts of black wings.
Your dark corpse awes
Our high diffusing eyes: on desert sands
Stirred by no breath
Sharply it decays. From rising heat it draws
Quick silent quill-
Tipped wings far down its deep vortex in chill
Steeped narrowings.

In the Habiliments of a Dead Friend

Snakes leave their skin and live;
No figured leaf-skin, theirs, to give
Some after-Edenite
A change of hiding from the sight
Of God. Snakes won that right.

Though naked was your birth,
One final suit you took to earth.
Habit holds the dead
Still; dust may be well-bred
If once inhabited.

The coat you used to wear
Allays my fear of going bare.
Death's empty hieroglyph
Is your shape to this shell. What if
I grow, as it is, stiff?

A Prayer

O God,
Lift me to such abode?
Me, awash in the blood
Of the limb,
My unwiped barnyard feet
Indelible with sweet
Manure?
What soul can sit untainted
In so strong a world?
Restrain
To what no thing is pure,
Dreamed of, removed, not so
That one
Heaven of concept cool
As inner ice, for use
Below
After the sting of none
Or sweat of too much love.